# Poetry is for Sissies

*by Arthur Weil*

# Poetry is for Sissies

## Copyright © 2000 by Arthur Weil

For all inquiries or to order additional copies of this book, contact Arthur Weil, 208 Pala Avenue, Piedmont, CA 94611, aweil444@aol.com
Pricing: $5 per copy, 5 or more $4 each plus postage & handling

Some images copyright www.arttoday.com

ISBN: 0-9676149-2-9

Printed in the U.S.A. by BookMasters, Inc.

# *Dedication*

I would like to dedicate this book to all of the wonderful service organizations throughout the United States. The Lyons, Rotary Clubs, Shriners, but most of all to the 330,000 International Kiwanis organizations. They help develop parks, feed the hungry, visit the ill in hospitals, build playgrounds and improve local schools and the lives of children everywhere.

These service organizations efforts to improve our local communities through voluntary services are not only a tremendous offering but a true gift from the heart. It is a practice in the essence of humanity, brotherhood and friendship.

Thank you so much for all you do and will do.

# Acknowledgments

To Sasha Gottfried for reviewing, proofing and editing.

*Special thanks to Seth Lepore for the excellent work in compiling, editing, and arranging this self-published book. Your consistent generosity, dedication and humor are more than appreciated.*

# Table of Contents

## *Photo/ Sketch Art Credit*

Front Cover Photo, Arthur Weil on beach near Santa Cruz, 1955
*For You*, p.1, Photo of Charlotte Kaufman, Arthur's mother (1939)
*The Player*, p.3, Painting by Degas
*Parting*, p.4, Statue by Emanuel Vigeland, Oslo, Norway
*The Devil Did It*, p.13, Sketch by Arthur Weil
*Meditative Thought*, p.15, Statue outside Tokyo, Japan
*Secrets*, p.18, Sketch by Donna Mendez
*Love Me Lillian*, p.24, Photo of Lillian Weil
*Once in a While Stop*, p.27, Painting by Andrew Wyeth
*Naked*, p.31, Painting by Georges Rouault
*Wisdom*, p.34, Photo of foliage at the Lake Merritt Gardens
*Encourage*, p.40, Statue by Emanuel Vigeland, Oslo, Norway
*Grieving*, p.43, Photo, Scotland
*Action Theater*, p.49, Photo, Halloween, Piedmont, CA
*Evaporate*, p.56, Photo, Lake Tahoe
*Fled the Nest*, p.57, Photo, Cabo San Lucas, Mexico
*Let the World In*, p.59, Photo, Maui, Hawaii
*Do What's Right*, p.66, Photo of yellow rose, Piedmont, CA
*Ride of Life*, p.71, Waterpark, Reno, NV
*Day's End*, p.75, Photo, Cabo San Lucas, Mexico
*Puzzle*, p.82, Photo, National Gallery, Washington, D.C.
*Innocence of Youth*, p.84, Photo of Josh and Ben Steinhorn, Ixtapa, Mexico
*Real or Fantasy*, p.91, Painting by Fernand Léger
*Revolution*, p.92, Photo of crowd gathered in front of Bill Clinton, Oakland, CA, 11/3/2000
*Other Side of Happiness*, p.99, Photo, Saint Lucia, Caribbean
*Leaving Footprints*, p.101, Photo of Lillian Weil, Carmel beach, CA

## *For You*

I welcome you
With love and open arms

Much is primitive, simple, diluted
Polluted

Just to read
To nurture the mind
For that I love and thank you

Some of my rhymes may touch
A raw nerve
Some interactive
Some close and dear
Evoke a smile, a chuckle or a tear

I love and thank you
You are the winner
Internalize,
Feel like the winner of a special prize

Joyous, exploratory
Adventurous beginner

## *Stages of Life*

The babe's head purple, struggling
Flesh torn born
Into a challenging world
Each stage in life
The heavens and the earth unfurled

Why curious, conscious
Brief innocence helpless

Defensive   excessive   cautious
Always learning   absorbing   questioning
Mating   binding   nurturing family and friends
Growing little knowing
Optimism   realism   new directions

Extroversion and introspection
You wonderful wonderful world

It is through knowing pain that joy enthralls
It is failure that brings hope, driving force
Out of the mean new value our goodness and success
It is through silent, lowly prayers
Infallible or rational belief, in spirit's awe
So blessed

## Life's Angle

Life has an angle, a hook to it
Everything seemed so perfect
Yet I blew it
One wrong word
One wrong move
One deed

Erased, chased
The world with its ever new twist
All the healing,
All the warmth dissipated, missed
Man, woman, too complex
ego is riled, jealousy
Hurt   undercut   harmony lost its fit

Disarray
Anger, frustration have their way
Over one not-so-stupid misdeed
Misunderstood, overreacted, our feelings bleed
Flow of hatred, impulses hurt
Brain waves pulsating
Blood does spurn
We hit, we beat
We yell out loud, repeat
When the shout
Free, is now out

We do reflect
Now our intellect asks why?

Why did I so violently react?
Reject
When bonds of love, friendship were so dear
One word, one deed
The mind emotes deep disappointment does appear
Not questioning the self     why?
A trust never broken
Faith betrayed by act and lie
Only time, reason turns the human wheel
To mend    to heal
Out of pain and wisdom born anew
Share new life,
Wonder why we say hurtful things  and do
Are really part of life that's true
I'd rather not blow it
Apologize and show it
Spoken rudely out of turn
Will I ever learn?

## The Player

Will the spirits open our hearts?
Shuffle, deal, play winning cards
Fate can spite me the "chooser"
Play an honest game
Must have a winner and loser

Play it often, play it well
It's in the game, the sport
The player's nature you can tell
If per chance you lose
Blame it on the court
Life's exciting new game you choose

Alert, clever    cautious make your move
Watch out for regulation rules, behoove
Play your optimum best
Love and nature's hormones do rest

Playing center court not for the weak
Adrenaline – competitive I seek
Protagonist each throw or blow
Win for points, for honor, ego all I know

Better to play with loving partner now
For in love's nature, no restraints
Do what your conscious does allow but
Be careful of the devil and the saints

No guilt, no heart feeling, no shame
Some say it's just a game

## *Parting*

I am tired
She said, he said
It's the feelings to be weighed
Cannot change them so assayed
Tender nerves of love and heat
Arteries pump, nerves telegraph pain

I berate you
You in me engrained
I do not hate you
Strong words of parting
Our stubborn egos
Strong, uncompromising
Do we never learn, never smartin'

Each time we meet, rejoice
Soon sparks misunderstood
Words, like poison tentacles dart

Exert excruciating pain
Confuse and fill our brain with
Stop, no more, please not again, seize delay
A frolic subject now black and negative
Tired of fighting and the fray
Instead inhale perfume
Numbed is the avid fragrance of the day

The green, the rose, the yellow pink in bloom
The canvas all about a splendid canvas I assume
But, alas, all is not what it seems
Long shattered our dreams

Divorce, parting, so painful
Our misunderstandings torrent more than rainfall
Love    hate    succumb
Your refusal empties heart with tender feelings numb
Deep love, infatuation makes me weak
I will succumb to rejoin you
If you but ask and seek
If in stubbornness and arrogance
I'll float out there with others to take a chance
You quench my flame, you make me sweat
I'll distance in our parting never to forget
You


## *Too Little Too Much*

Disseminate my thought
Positive, altruistic, caring
Of love, goodness and worth
My poetry of life preparing

Most will agree
Critic's opinion some of you may curse
He dissects your words as only he can see
Puts you in a hearse

Your phrases glow
Like emeralds and rubies
Glisten and shine most admirably
Testify of things that are improving
Our world is getting better

The critic says not true
Society, downtrodden sadder
You say mild temperature, the air is pure

Earthlings busy under an azure sky
Critic will dig and contort, twist reason
Frown, see dark clouds way up high
The weather this year out of season

The food, festive music, celebration by the score
The critic says: *So what, we had that all before*
*It's all so primitive, it's just a bore*

Wonderful museum now constructed
Retort: *wasted tax money deducted*

New inventions race in space
What good doomsayer
Fall on our face
Laugh and joy and celebrate

Why waste time, money
Too many other things needed in our nation

Music too loud
Cars too fast
Jet plane noise unhealthy TV blast
Genetic foods
Elective representatives
Limited taxation
Storage of oil
Some good must ration
Too many divorces
Babies out of wedlock
Poor teachers

When will we wake up
Take stock?

America's uneven scale
The good outweighs the bad by ton and bale
Our system with its weakness
Its faults in seasoned freedom
Surpasses most past civilization
Modern gadgets, better medicine
More security than our forefathers
Have ever seen
Despite homeless, drugs
Exhibition, little prohibition

Crime, disease, hunger
In decline and in attrition

Each year improve our comfort zone
Wise enough, convert, do atone
Seem to live 3 lives in 1
Despite the effort, stress
With thrive and build
Have lots of fun

We do have hope
Have faith
For our children
The human race
Often I wonder:
When can I get off this place?


## Creative Brain...

now neutral    lame

fatigue, exhaust

too much, too fast    to blame

yet we live asleep and latent
the myriads of strands

in cells
that we call brain

we live        sustain

G
O
D
S

magic brain computer
simply turns neuter

rest, reflex, reborn
my brain soon will blow

it's horn

soon restore    pinnacles    of extradition

just patience until I reclaim

my new born will

## Combat Ready

Gladiators do not bed women
Prior to a fight
It drains their spirit
Soothing, after battle seek delight

So better not
Save, anxious for combat
Win and victory in sight
All nerves zero in
One zeal to beat, to win
Such narrow but perceptive goal
Impregnated in my body and my soul
Assures the greatest strength and concentration

Combat ahead, all muster participation
Ready for the war sensation
Ironic, that man, victorious glorious
Has secret needs
Nourishes inner strengths
Must again defeat

Thoughts often meaningless
That is our culture
The nature of sneers
Prepared and trained
First have the gift    be full brained
To please the mob, festering masses
Biased, primitive – bordering on asses
The nature of the human beast to fight
That doesn't make it right!
Man does constantly bathe in new creation
Steadfast to defend his station

# Platitudes

Life is destined      rushing through an open gate
Innocent exciting, terror, love and fate
It's the moment, glimpse, the smile
Angelic look, the love shared with me now
And for a while

Erase the anxious face
Grasp, cling to good thoughts ever near
Engrain the brain with rich and witty text
Stop      slow down      question
Where am I going                next?

Charming music stimulates feelings of grandeur
The sight of laughing children anxious to play more

The spirit succumbs, last gasping breath
The soul all whole is resurrected
Macabre dance of eternal life and death
Why?
Sensitive, provoking touch, tenderly transmitted
Yours to give and receive is well befitted

The help of a friend
Patience to understand
Everything rapport so treasured
Goodness giving never measured

Each of us is an island in a sea of
Humankind

Attack and merge
With partners that we find
Climb from the abyss of despair
To greener grasses, sunshine everywhere

Must do and act far more than cope
In our action, deeds transform reality and hope
Climb on the transportation information age
Elevate our knowledge upwards at an even stage

Yet all of us at times will slip and stumble
Misjudge, misguided blind, we fumble
Devils like hate, envy can bring us to despair
Our very human nature will soon heal

Nourished, reawakened we soon strive

Time, leave too soon
You have but one life

Be daring, brace yourself, do share your gift
Unique, creative that you are
Give yourself a well-deserved lift
Venture leaving your narrow box
Push obstacles and rocks
Like Hercules collect gargantuan power
Morals, values, deep belief espouse and tower
Let no man thwart your dream
Within us nurture the G'd given power so supreme

You can feel it
Sense and reel it
Live so short
Rest test after test
Join and participate
Amongst all is the pang of love
Stirring embers of desires is our fate

Right now you    who must feel
Know that you are heavenly blessed
World gates wide open
Dare take the test


## Aging

As you go over the 70th or 80th year threshold
The inevitability of death is overwhelming
Whether conscious or suppressed
The short life-span left is like
A reverse sentence of living

In youth our sight ahead
Work and play advance
All excited
Future without limit
No ceiling
Free choice & daring
The tide, the scale tipped
Suddenly health and age collide

We weren't supposed to live to 70 or 90
Or 100
Life vs. existence, that is
Our nursing homes are full

Taxed to the brim
With broken bodies
Hanging on a string of hope

It is the bridge between the last years
Of self-propelling life
Versus intuition that is frightening
Unprepared, especially when friends die
Become incapacitated

I am walking such a tight rope
In the abyss, alert objective
Love to write
Shudder to waste
Time on non-essentials left to help
Since I earned and saved and deserve some
Of the help
I am lucky
It's still an adventure


## Drained

ever feel so tired,        so down
                    mentally drained
that standing on the precipice
            the abyss of utter despair

one tiny push...

over the cliff into eternal oblivion
            no one seems to care

forlorn   lonely   isolated
        Little     hope
                        no strength

it doesn't matter
            about the final
end

nothing matters  down    down

everything always reduced to

                nothing (ness)

It happens only once                    in a while

## Living Alone On Love

When you leave
Last hug and sensuous kiss
Sadness and joy as they compound
The door shuts, isolates
Your profile, your sound
Your radiant fragrance, eyes divine
Treats my competitors
So please decline
Stay mine

Next conversation teasing
On the phone so pleasing
Repartee, relate, raucous
Daring is our tone
All geared up for next delicious rendezvous
When in private embrace
We are the liberated two

Yet more divided
Love potion yes, much else so undecided
Days and lonely nights
Each tender, hopeful conversation lifts
To higher sights
Why do the lovers blindly nourish
Yet seek more
I live alone on love
With hormones, longing yet in store
Ecstasy, touch with embrace I most adore
Impetuous, must I dim the fire
Is it unreasonable to thirst for such desire?


## Rationalize

In the name of right
We can rationalize
Right supercede by might
Must have at its premise
The ten commandments
Including thou must not kill
Innocently regardless of war rules

# The Devil Did It

You say there is no devil
I say there is
Tempting, devious
Breaking the will
Testing mores

Go be lecherous
With desire
Eat, eat- obesity deformed
Waste, watch TV
Heathen celebrate
Cheat, lie, cover up - devil's work
All the time the battle- good vs. evil
Desire vs. restraint
In the silence of the night
Extra drink, extra pill
Destroyed, momentarily the will
Black magic, magnet
Pulled into a false world
A world of hate, deception
While fighting back

Innocent witness
With a floating docility, vacillation
I overstep

From purgatory to hell
The underworld absorbs,
Swallows up the only children
Pray to heaven
Extol the power of nature
Regurgitate
Nourish your will
With strength and determination
Balance the light from the dark
Open conscious eyes

Blinding torrent into the rational
Dew and dim world of today

13

Purge- the addiction sets in
No to extra pills
No to unhealthy meal
No to wasteful urge, foolish spending
No to the extra glass of alcohol
Be not blasphemous- refrain
Only goodness in word and deed
Sustain

The devil made me do it
Maybe he did and emptied my soul
Repair it – make the misshapen, whole
In faith, belief
Beg for reprieve
It will come
It WILL come

## We Lost

I had to let her go
It was too painful
Each tear of love
Bruised deep into my head
She too in pain
Close experience
Cleaved in two
Who would soon part

We said too much
Too freely
Loved too much
Obsession and rejection
As dear old friends are apt to do
In the fractious thought
Issue is taken
Stand taken
Ground taken
Where love and friendship connected two

No doubt, misunderstanding
Demanding retreat
The rhetoric replete
With accusation
She was so beautiful
We had so much going for us
She was determined not to give in
And lost
I lost too

## *Meditative Thought*

No matter how poor or rich
Tonight before eyes close
Escape your niche
Meditate
Reflect
Pray
With dignity
Inquire, self-respect

In a corner of your room
Where peace, compassion now does loom
Silently eyes open or close
Relax, breathe heavy out of mouth and nose
In contrast to the litany of hectic day
The power of the spirit now holds sway

Imagine jewels, rings, coins your life's treasure
Gone, nothing to lose
Material wealth replaced not choose
Prophetic inspiration of your "Id"
This moment is yours to make your bid
You left an aching soul
Reborn in nature, feel so whole
No interdiction, no restriction

Just being free to move in space and thought
Kindred the company and love sincere not to be bought
Spontaneous, generous – bodies of beaming new-made friends
Supportive, caring, no pretense

Dream-like peruse salve for your cures
Contraction angels mixed with whores
Unfurled nourished sustained, new venues now unfurled
Confusing aspects of our more macabre world
Tired, utter fatigue, I now retreat almost asleep

Timeout, at ease, a covenant to keep

Which virtue won
Which temptations now undone
I close my eyes, I yawn
Weaker, tired feel almost like a pawn
One aspect: sleep ignore
The other: face the spirit to the core
Were food, the clothes soon to disappear
Stripped of my outer garments,
I am what I am still here

Tomorrow strict feelings
Of weight and won and dealings
Of this day I help the poor
Did I take time to listen
Did I improve the world an iota more
Did I love and share love
Did I uplift and was uplifted
My human touch with imbeciles so gifted
Did I study, read, learn
Lose my inhibitions hope and yearn
Did I repay my bets or debts

Oh wondrous day
Before I fall asleep
Wish me, protect me
Good vibrations I must keep

## Ordinary

The ordinary can grow beastly, powerful and overwhelming
Concocted in my mind, a fright, a monster at it's helm
Until wisdom's jewel
Does overpower
If we dissect, attack the fear
Eventually, becomes ordinary once again

# Time

Youth, you see with open eyes the aged
Stooped, wrinkled as they shove by
So withered worn
No one can deny their tired eyes reflect
Feelings, passions much like yours
Of love, hope and envy
A life to understand
Digesting bombardment of daily avalanche, of news
His membranes, pathos, feelings deep
Friendship, tenderness, hope
Prayer of loneliness
Exuberance is rare
So is depression
Dressing, eating, walking, pills, washroom
Unsure, suspicious, alert bent head steady
Hold on to few material things, what's left
They mean less and less each day

Think young one
Where is your priority
See his wisdom between the crags
His stubbed face, weight of history behind
Your benefits and letdowns were his creation
What do you have?
He hasn't luck and
Time

Can you see yourself at 70 or 85?
No, neither could I
And I am still alive

# I Can See Him

half-mast     a death

   remembrance                                    last      breathe

     I, human                    do reflect

thank  G'd     that us he did select

       to rationalize

            to idolize

our thoughts to synthesize

daily ventures   a surprise

I remember his face

his grace

his uncensored and stern decisions

I can see him in front of me

now he is gone and yet he lives

## *Secrets*

Hidden secrets entombed in our mind
Chained, fortress to our being blind
Our first love, overwhelming crush
Sexual repression, dreamlike on the rush

Secret undiscovered, item in our possession
Absconded, daring an obsession
Knowledge, deep confided by a friend
Fright returned that will never end

Secret in the family privy to us few
Secret of the dying friend I knew
Secret of my hope and fears wake me when visions now appear

Secrets of the heart
When recall a painful bull's eye with a dart
Secrets festered, do not seize
Do not ask me to reveal     please

# Man's Self Destruction

Genetics and mutation seeds within our soil
Creators of new wealth, food and foil
Society – so affluent, so full of wealth
Latest computers, gadgets, stealth

Yet, blind, learned hatred eats into flesh
Like poison, hopeless, vile and fresh
Reverse evolution is the game
Jealousy, envy fame
Arrogant cousins to the villainous
A deadly feeling called hatred
Better to die and be reborn than sustain
Rather than perish as subhuman beast
As mankind's' scorn, dead and deceased

Born, no. Before Adam and Eve
No reprieve
The world already in transition and turmoil
Earth's circumference did boil and roil

Born in innocence, in agonizing pain
Years of famine, floods and rain
Travail, false mental implants
Confusion, twist will of destruction
Each failure grows into uncertain experience
Valleys and mountains chiseled new production

Emotion overtakes reason
Animalistic overshadows the human intellect
No belonging, loyalty, all is treason
Thunder, lightning, death gains respect

Intellectually destructive
Implant or clone
Imbalance we are open prone
Animal, transformed creature
Full of hate
Where is truth
Command of Good and Evil

Ours a road of self-destruction
We all have a right to hate
A right to live, stand firmly without suction
The genesis of mutation, monster or genius

To tinker with new gods of introduction

More production, more destruction
Too late for consequences
Yet no choice –
It's never too late
The ozone, heated earth,
Species disappearing
Mutations gone awry
Acid lakes, acid clouds
Contamination, pests,
Unrealistic expectations
Lust and distrust
Land erosion
Population explosion
Glued to the Palm or computer
Grotesque, life extended

Is cosmos rainbow's beauty all for naught?
Where is the ray of hope?

## Somebody

I felt I was nobody
I know that not to be true
For you are dear
That makes an even two

## Ancient Men...

Knew ancient war wise
That is why we shy away
From ancient man
His wisdom
Love of nature, life
With closed eyes

## June Solstice

Solstice, the 21$^{st}$, the longest day
So beautiful     sunny
Green leaves, flowers bloom to stay
Colorful butterflies, bees hurry, busy, suck their honey

Yet, this longest day of light
Just as busy as the day before
Routine of duty, chores, love late at night
Earnings, buying from the store

Sounds boring, trite
One foot before the other
No time to think of future bright
Just do your duty mother

Summer days relaxed
To frolic, read, see nature's sign
To swim, hike, love's luscious perplexed
Touch dreams, imagine and feel divine

## Hormones

In youth the hormones will launch
The mind with endless vision of sex
In old age similar, but more complex
Where will I go, what will I eat today
Like child of 10 – I am supposed to play.
Sometimes I feel – that sex still here – is real

## More Lies

Eyes closed perceived the show
Vision images profound
A busy demanding world I see all around
Then I must open more lies

# Power of Words

Words are simply not enough

Each letter, each vowel, each invitation
Creeps on flowing, weaving sound waves
Audible the letter the word the thought
Jumps from end to station
Overwhelmed, sound silent smooth
Deafening
Staccato, halting
Sometimes singing
Supposed language we all speak
What if they babble Greek?

Is it the words in a sentence fused
Stir up feelings of anger or amuse
The speech prophetic
Is man's projection of deity inspired thought
Magnetic power or weak impulse
Control through work command, cajole
So stereotyped
Better now refrain

The words in sentence linked
Transmuted, more spiritual than tempting message
Work translated to thought, reflection or an order
Speech digested by another border

The impending power of each thought
Transmitted and received
Cannot be bought

The message long or short
Effective weak will soon abort
Words of hate, of kill
Strong impression
No need to distill
Yet buried love or help
Own intonation
We respond in many ways
On many levels
Yet each message on a dart
Bullet or computer chip
If heard
Gains some response

No man is an island to himself
Words flow physically
So sincere a request
Come pray with me
Telegraphed special
Hit the fuming bone
Of curiosity and atonement
Forgive wish praise
Is the child tantrum any dearer
Than a grown up

Are you listening?


## *Revolt*

Break habit, break routine
Conventions disappear
Not to be seen
Turn thought sideways and upside down
Laugh, smile, smirk and sometimes frown
Invent, create new points of view
Discard much of what you knew
Adventurous creative thought, a fresh approach
All mankind flexible, changeable, is what you coach

New mores, out of the womb – now so alone
Shed guilt, misleading habit formed in stone
Analyze duty and responsibility, debt
Mesh rainbow colors into masterpiece instead

I now awake, mere thought of change
I lived, I did, to change now is mighty strange
Yet I feel chained, in a mold so queer
Naked, reborn in a new world will appear
The tastes, the sound, the colors so glorious
New clothes, new venture most uproarious

Please let me go to a new, unfettered world
Where flags of pure freedom, poor madness are unfurled
Let me be the unborn newness, help shape the universe
Pour a golden rain of happiness out of my empty purse

Yet free and revolutionary men take their own advice
Win their destiny and hope, a blessing in disguise

## *Love Me Lillian*

Love me-not for my looks
Love me- not for my wealth
Love me for being
For seeing
For sharing
For caring

Love me to ease my pain
Love me for the laughter we share again
Love me for the memories of the past
Love me for our tenderness, hold me fast
For mind pictures transferred
For unspoken spirit that binds
For knowledge partaken of all kinds

For meals we shared
For prayers we prayed
For funerals attended
Never mended

For short temper
For my shortcomings
For presents small and big

Love each touch a present

Love me for my eyes open and closed
Vision
Premonition
Wrong decision
Recognition

Love me for my uncertainty
My worry
Impatience always in a hurry

Love me
For looking at the moon
Massage tender, licks and swoon
Love me for our trip on earth did end so soon

Love me for the things in me untouchable
Forgiving, unquenchable, such able
For my heart about to burst in laugh and pain
For the tranquil beauty next to storm and rain
Love me for who I am
As I throw, stretch arms to heaven
As our friendship bakes and leavens
At the troth of life we drink
Animalistic child at play, no time to think

Love me for the mirror sure to burst upon our scene
Love for the earth, music pure sweet and clean
Loud and boring, tempo pace
For my clumsiness and human grace
Love me for who I am
With world and you, comprise a tiny space
Our world so small and big, forever a new place

Love me as we wish posterity, life's joy
As we struggle to maintain oblivious and coy
Each seek the attainable forever changing dream
As we grow older, knowing things are never
what they seem

Love me for the sleep of sleeps
Eternal that we share
Love me for my love for you
precious always,  spare

Love me for the burst of lightning, thunder
thrashing furiously
As we hide, protect and wonder, will we
survive and spin most curiously

Love me for each beginning, wonder
must it end
Love me, I am what I am
Forever live eternal friend

## Interchange

As you crawl into my brain
So I worm into yours
Photo and sound our contact view
Mysteriously absorbed
Part of you and you of me
Impression and reactions
Stimulate meaning
Stir our senses
Play it by the ropes
Perceived, conceived and seized up
Mentally involved

With openness we absorb
Reflect, digest and test
Not agree, not believe
But influenced and peeved

*It's dark and cold outside*
*Can I come inside the house with you?*

First sentence of the night
Paragraph of two people
With fermenting, jelling chemistry
Other is close enough
Interesting, absorbing

The impression lingers on
Discipline our senses

Still the interchange between two
Is beyond measure
The mystic friendship turn to unison
Is questioned
We'll know
When we meet again

## *Once In A While Stop*

once in a while
stop what you do
stop

stop
close your eyes      reflect
open up your spirit and your  intellect
seek  truth
in silent meditation
nirvana one step nearer
put the world aside
emotions mushroomed with elation
like onion skin
the levels peel
newness  revealed
thankful, transformed
you'll feel
deep breath
slow   slowly   more rest
continue back to doing
new adventure, challenge brewing
know      life will be different from now on


## *Get To Know Her*

She's a tomboy
Full of muscle, springy and bright
Such a delight
Get to know her, you'll be thrilled
All your fears and apparition stilled

Just like you so full of zest
Each exciting hours face a test
Know, adore
Like you, find out and explore
She's so much more

## Pests

for days the pests
                would leave their nest

I tried to catch them
        invariably
                    I'd miss the

            zigzag                          pest


I am so elated

        I fumigated


the flying creature no more, gone
I won

                                                    (or did I?)

I have so proclaimed
                    do miss their activity


        instead
                                        it's their demise, they


            are gone



I am here instead

goodnight          restful in bed

goodbye

                        not so sweet
                                pests

# Overcome

How on such a sunny
Perfect cloudless day
Can I feel dismal anyway
Jubilee cheer the flowers, nature's bloom
Sad news, there's doom
Gnawing inside
A lack of hope, a plane of blight

Emotion bottled
Sickness of best friend
Gloomy downturn never ends
The product I created
Rejected and negated
*You stepped on my toe*
*And now I hate you so*

So with bright sun rays
A crisp cool, pleasant breeze
To me this is one of my dark days
With nothing more to please
Than nighttime, sleep may heal
Recoil the negative and bad news seal
The bee just buzzed full of new nectar
The birds' song cooed to one expect her
The day ahead rings glorious delight
But darn it when you feel like I do
Feelings overwhelm    change day to night

I stand up
Exorcise the demon full of blight
In calm now meditate on last week's great success
Becoming a believer once again, receive the blessing

I am alive with the latest gadgets at my beck and call
Things and more things
I have them all

In front of mirror I loosen up my facial frown
Tap dance and jump, be person about town
So what if dark clouds rain bad news
All of us occasional victims of the blues
There has to be a down if there's an up
Our failure strengthens our appreciation
How can we measure pain felt on so many levels

Of utter joy, jubilation grown out of sweat
Tears with laughter as an antidote
Of hate, misunderstanding when lovers win


## Reward Myself

This cookie buttery laced is my reward
New computer, gigantic four screened TV
New shoes, suit, gadgets of every kind and sort
No accolade, congratulation – simply my reward to me

You ridicule, you cast a hiss
Don't give a damn, lick or piss
Most critical of me, so full of doubt
To you my life a failure and a route

I, so victorious like Hercules could move the mighty boulders
Success, smile, pat myself with pride on both shoulders
Dexterous, with elegance I prance on air
Cause I feel proud, I made it care

Reflected and erect, injected with accomplishment
Served, nerve, reaped well earned wealth
In stocks or money, shiny things I do not resent
But most in feeling, full blood, proud God given health
In common with the royalty and kings

Smile now from cheek to cheek
With dancing heart at eagle's peak
I find myself, I finish what I started
I added, helped, see fruition not yet parted

Compliments, handshakes in life's upper atmosphere, so rare
Highly motivated, simply chart my way, pay my own fare
I'm busy, self-content and of the happy grouchy sort
For mine the world, the pinnacle, horizon on my own accord

I owe you world and you owe me
I used you and you used me
From clay and elements with a touch of life
I've bounced, consumed rip roaring rife

So what, so when, so now that counts
The dance of death far distant haunts
Join me who made it in a thousand ways
Let us love live in great unison until the end of days

## Today

If suddenly the premonition of my death
Comes, do I
More or less cry
End all in pain
Angry, say good bye to the world

It will come soon
Too soon
For those of us who love life
Love the freshness of the morning
Love soft, mushy kisses tantalize
Don't want to leave few friends
The magic full moon
Eaten up by worms, bugs
Skeleton no more to feel, not me!

There is today!
There is now!

## Naked

Naked
Too late, alone
Shoes, stockings
Disrobe, stark naked
Sit here, write

Mind directs the hand
No matter how naked
Covered in robe poetic

Chaotic, overdressed world
That someday must strip down
To feel its roots

Cosmos cooled, born as fireball
Start on sheer nakedness
No shame, lost in nature
Until, magic breath of life spirited
Suddenly, dressed, a person
Approaches and like a foreigner
Showers distrust, confusion and anxiety
Where there was pure bliss and innocence
All was good and perfect
The mind has no place
To retreat
Expresses the ultimate of love and anger

Naked
To fight for its existence
In the name of humanity


Our body projects to places
The toes hairy
Our sexual glands disjointed aberration
Necessary, most peculiar
Turn off the moon and sun

Let me out again
Be my naked self
For I am no better
No worse
I will sleep and die that way

I feel variety
Parts of my body
Each so different
Each reaction so original
I see my body, naked, in matter
Like an ambidextrous creature
From inner space
That I am

All the parts
So delightfully their own
No thought of selfishness, of narcissism
For all is me, selfish and ego driven
For whom do I sit naked

At the edge of the bed
Powerless, helpless, fettered
Human or very inhuman
Each naked member of a complex
Sophisticated species

As my naked body moves
Walks and runs in motion
Part of the universe, moves with it
The overdresses, over-colored
Overbuilt world

Where are your roots, man?
Where is your heritage, your dignity?
To persevere is clothe it, the cold
I would forgo clothes like
A three year old who wants
Total naked abandonment

Even my mind is often better off naked
Instead of being crammed, confused
Help me! I am still in need
Help me, keep my faith and sanity
Be a human being

## *Wake Early*

wake early
too early

workers     ready

        eyes barely     open

                what?

duty jobs chores...

uneasy feelings in my pores

     not washed,     or showered

feel pressured

            (coward)

let me at least

                              brush my   teeth


                    is this what life is about?

yesterday        my choice

now fret                                    pout


          things will improve each hour
                    or will they?


                    *Wisdom...*

Is in sharing the best of your
          Experience
Chuckling at your past
          Mistakes and imperfection
Knowing
          Life is flux
There is always something new
          To learn
Most of us have to learn
          By failure, experience
The hard way
          Time the healer and destroyer
Will whisper
          Doubt
Your inner sanctity
          Will feel the unsure answer
Is wisdom to know better
          Or to omit judging the impossible

For sometimes it is best not to know
          To admit mistakes, ignorance
Shed arrogance replaced by humility
          To know your day will come and end


                    34

# The Epistle

Love   deep undivided
          for my fellow man
Love   for now, for a life span
Love   for a babe, so innocent
          changing by day
Love   with a stranger
          until he went away
Love   understanding, understanding
          parceled out
Love   vibrant hostile ending in
          a rout
Love   tender touching full of sensation
Love   dazzling, tingling, full of vibration
Love   from a distance admired
Love   from defeat surrounds still inspired

Love   for the special dead
          for mourning eternally few
Love   overcoming hate, mate and envy
          no competition
Love   in disguise as ghost
          an eternal apparition
Love   hanging on a string
Love   the ear, nostrils
          the mouth should sing
Love   of those less fortunate in squander
          stupor, hanging humiliated
Love   of the light and day
          all the shadow in between
Love   as a veil, a hidden curtain
          this special service
          written in the sky or sand
Love   in that eternal magic bond
          between life and nature
          a spirit enveloped with
          the sanity of life

Love   is the extension to connect
          the physical love for touch and pleasure
          the emotional love
          the bond between mother and child
          family and friend
          the willingness to give one's life

```
          for the earth, the land
          in which you live

Love    for oneself
          in our gloom
          in our speech
          in our zest for life

Love    for our heritage
Love    for our globe, the earth
          but a speck, reflection in the
          unending universe unlimited

Love    even in pain sickness
          grieving, in loss of almost all
          there is the love of moment
          the love of tomorrow
          in dream, in vision

Love    reaching out, sensitivity
          from mind to heart
          every sensitive fiber
          for we are all formed in the image
          deformed, different, peculiar
          creatures, each with our own
          thoughts, aspirations
          yet imbued from birth
          with the magic of love
```

## *You Can Make It*

He who says *You'll never make it*
Astute, evaluate
You can take it

Diligent in fortitude
Study, plan
Your interlude
You conceive your plan
Because you can

Learn, practice
Go, it's yours to do
Your action, your belief

Do not forsake
Unless you really try
You'll never know if you can make it
Earned your share of the pie

## *Crippled*

Wings cut
I am a cripple. Both of us are cripples
For Christ's sake we were born whole
Sucked on our mother's nipple

Productive
Decades flee by so fast
Until broke, declined at last
Our thrust diminished
Yet here, we are far from being finished
We love, cherish hours and days
Observe pain is the game we play
It's now that counts instead a fast distrustful way

Our wings are cut
Eyes still can see, ears listen, and the nose inhales
Yet the old heart heavenly pumps it back
I, crippled, follow your truth and wisdom

Banner of hope
The sick and poor do cope
Perchance you move and far depart
I miss you truly with an open heart

Who has a notion
Of shift and pendulum emotion
Nothing stands still
Nor ever will
An unfair, most exciting world
To leave, to die is the great sin
Too much to live for
Too much humor, competition
Creative, spinning mind
Decides by indecision

## Destitute

I am a fifty-ish sexy broad
Was married several times
In Vegas as a showgirl sought
Musician husband married me
With other women repartee
And threw me out

Temporary job in office, homeless
All in storage, a few suitcases I here possess
Some old guy let me use the sofa in his house
Tonight I was late, so he locked me out
I sit in a booth at the coffee shop near by
Robbed of my self-esteem, lost, can't even cry
Where will I sleep? How to meet the morn?
Have a few coins, disheveled, a bit torn

I call this guy. Can almost see he shakes his head
Afraid to mess with me, might drown him in his bed
"I need $50 for the hotel room for the night
Can you get it to me? I'll be all right."
A torrent of words on phone, words of despair
How did I get this way? Where to go. Where?

I have no children in this town, no pets
Abysmal stupidity on my part, lots of regrets
"You say you'll come, get me a room?
Even a dirty one, I feel I'm in a tomb."

"I just need a few more weeks to earn more
So I can leave with bucks in store."
"I had this accident, pain in my brain
Sometimes I get so lost, almost insane.
It's 12:10 am, when will you be here?"
Ten minutes he said, lessened my fear

He brought me $50 cash – someday I will repay
Drove me to the motel a couple blocks away
It's 12:35 am at the over-priced room
A good bath, safe for the night I do assume
The old man nice, rejected my treat
I may be broke, but have something that men need

Don't blame him scared with all my plight
Could mess his life up for a visit in the night
I still have charm, a busty broad
In olden times, men felt lucky if caught

38

He wished me luck, told me leave town, depart
Gave me hug, said: *Go away* with mixed uncertain heart

Five more days before the boss took me to Greyhound
Bus took me up north to family, they never made a fuss
I blame it on the accident and mine
Head injury they said, most times I do feel fine
Then again I didn't have a chummy fan
My ex–house in town, off limits and a ban
I'll get a bunch of money soon
I know it

I am taking the bus
Honestly, I'll leave and take the bust

It's now been months I haven't heard
Scammed his money,
He said, *Poor thing*
*They clipped your wings you wounded bird.*
I agree. They did


## Possibilities

The world isn't all
That it's cracked up to be
A world of opportunities for all time
An infinite world of possibilities
If you call putting a triangle
Into a square whole
Possibilities
It all depends on the open door
Who walks through it


## Last... (Fill-In)

I have nothing to_____
I ate all_____
This is your last_____

# *Encourage*

All of us need to be stroked
Tickled, cajoled, to be joked
To be humored, encouraged and prepped
Congratulated, helped and kept

We all belong
We carry a torch
Sing universal song

No sooner do succeed
Than we realize
We too are in deep need
We are ambitious, want to thrive
To play, serve, to be alive

Continuous spark from birth to now
Too busy, oblivious, blind, not know how
We procreate, impress and share
We rave, nourish and do care

Foremost self-fulfillment incomplete
We struggle, plan, amuse at time
Deceive ourselves for what we are about
To spend short time on earth determined, proud

Nature revolves in counterpoint
In our lives with all parties we are joined
Despite objection, surprising travel
Our own truth search does unravel

What we are and what we want to be
Is slowed with brakes, our goal to be absolutely free
Duty, family and health
Preclude limit, despite ambition, faith and wealth

So better take each hour, day
Let positive thought hold sway
Laugh heartily, smile, rejoice
Leave time to play with friends, make noise

The time of life ticks gone is the previous
Aging, natural, real and devious
Looking part rich, full of thirsty sip
Than a bum joy ride        but it was my trip

## *Writing the Truth?*

My rhymes not great

      but good

My pontification tiresome

      but true

My verbiage juxtaposition

      misunderstood

My reflection of life and death

      happiness and pain I know

I do admit

                      I
                do write

empty brain
soul        right by      your side

ebullient
     awkward     rich

          with humor, graphic        pride

    always honest

life so good
    or such a      bitch

# Marching

Mostly we slither, walk or crawl
Cajole, rejoice, blatantly bawl
This time we march
In unison
Though not in step
We march for justice, fairness
For moderation, not excess (unless)
For nature's preservation
Self-destructive, the planet's population
We march for babies loved and cared
For old, crippled pain diminished and spared
For science and research
Disease, arthritis we must purge

We march
For hope, for fair of fellow man
Fortuitous share our lifetime span
For less desire in material things
For feelings equal to the leaders and kings
For less vanity
For less insanity

We march
For the arts
The painter, poet, writer
Musician, singer, soul enlightened
For show of athletes great
We hail the icons, shout their fate
Icons with money riches
Dazzle us, performance stars
We adulate space, flight going off to Mars
These gifted heroes, ever trained in shape
For them, with them we march

Most of all we march for will and cause
Our belief balances better loves
Lucky in a sea of freedom's air
We can express, partake and dare
We are tiny ants on mankind's giant globe
The actors, protagonists of hope

We march
As symbols, flags of voice
We march to change society, provide some choice
We march to right some wrong

We know the world so small
Can be so much better

## Grieving

Why do I survive?
When dear one died, lost her life?
Why out of this human sea
It was she not me
Depraved, I am saved?

I know I'm lucky as I contemplate
My time draws nearer
Not ready yet for fate
She who shared my bed for
        Forty-four years
Left me,     empty in sorrow    wracked
        overwhelmed   with empty tears


Her heart has stopped – so soon - died in vain
        Enveloped by a myth, an aura to sustain
        If death is final, why do I see her face
        Full and firm, her body so distinct
Their spirit, love in memory does transcend

I feel her closeness, breath and voice
Their wisdom gesture, every pose
I want to touch again, softly adore
Declare one everlasting love

Where are you, let me kiss your inviting lips
Let me touch your fingers, your breast
        hips
Let me ask for forgiveness for not caring more

I admire, I love you
     You were the only one
     I adored

Now in this big house, great works
     I am so very alone
Studied, toiled was honest
     I atone
Said my prayers, blessed my fellow man
My life history, a time that only
     I can visualize and scan

## Adieu

Numbed by constant array of critique
The way you look, dress and eat
No pathos humor, I'm a dud
The cream of worthless glue of mud

So I perceive her wail, complaints
Link upon links I shudder at the devil's saints
Please one compliment, one kind word
With elocution style your criticism hurt

Pain of betrayal
Sadness drains
Face tired, pale
Heartbeat heavy brittle can sustain

A sense of onlyness
Lifeblood sucked in loneliness
No family that's close
No friends, all went, all goes

It is my words
My deeds knifed through like swords
Cut off the joy, the hope evaporated away
Now deep regret, made no amends to save the day

Now I feel so morose    gagged    forlorn
The world alive, it's me that I scorn
Raised my kids, let them fly free
Never nourished friends, now pay the fee

Sit at the edge of bed
Reflect, wonder, feeling sad
Will it get better

It must it must     yet I feel sadder

You my friend? In the name of self-righteous torture complaint
We built a chasm, more distant strained
Yet I love your charm, your beauty and your shape
I succumb no more, nod as your chimpanzee and ape

Comes early dawn
New challenge, opposition spawn
The daily puzzle, pieces missed
Have to be mended, loved and kissed

Like in an escalator, going up and down
One day a father, fool or clown
Next day the insular, selfish flea
Sucking, jumping, biting with glee

Fatigue, finish finally at last
Colorful mural of life depicts the past
When I awake the pressure's on
Each duty     deed     weighs like a ton

A little smile, accomplish much
A compliment, reward and such
A warm embrace, a kiss     just tender touch
I've made it long ago     now little things do mean so  much

I hate to let you go
Last act, a tragedy, it's curtain
End of show
Too bad, won't work, of that I'm certain


## Life Goes

Destroyed one
Replaced by another
Amoebae split
Life goes on
One buried almost forgotten
One active, one besotted
Birth, growth, mutation
The spiral cellular life
Temporary scanning
The temporal sphere
Determined, assured
Clouded in secrecy

## The Visit

After years old friend to visit
The bell rings
Years lost,
Deep anxious siren sings
So much to share, to say
Between us words reel off without delay

Deep feelings soon restored
A smile, a sigh, each answer underscored
Familiar, despite the dying years
Open, admit, share to touch, span time and silvery tears

Alas the friend must leave so soon
So I retrench with heart memories in my cocoon
How I remember

## Dare Me

I, the seed of seeds from Adam or before
I alive, searching this great earth
that I adore
I, a microcosm, grain amongst mankind living
Eager to meld, wide joy of giving

Dare me, care for me, spare me
Touch my life
Stir the juices, shapes
that I thrive
Now here is my moment, my time
Echo, mold and shape, I'm in my prime

The single chain of deeds that feeds
Work, fun and grieving all are meshed
Fox harvest gathers, shaken, thrashed
Here's to the fruit, the loot to suit

Stray not, disappoint me not, your seed now grieving
Put me on your pedestal, forever feeling
Great in need distrust, but still believing

## Macabre Omen

When we are most down

        Depressed, addicted alcoholic freak

Only one way up     or torture, trauma anchor down

        Friends, family, society forsaken

Maelstrom of the underworld, down hurled, hopeless

        A beaten animal, too late

Until death, demise and self-destruction

        Takes its expensive toll

If by death, balance overpopulation

        I say go back – no obituary

A history of patience, of sorrow

        Lost is the morrow – in sickly stupor

Life could get better    without help or hope – no way

        Dying, death    all disarray

Statistic, not missed, devils experiment of futile festivity

        Macabre omen of a sick society

Who will be next         (?)


## Old Ears

My old ears buzzing
I hear it distinctly
Over nothing
Except I can't be told
That years ago I was too old

## *Come Closer*

My eyes pursue your vision
Fogged, mystic indecision
Message from brain telegraphed to arm
My arm pointed like an arrow
To you so dear, so full of charm
Distant, yet so visible

Longer, longer the arm now slightly bent
In asking motion
Begs you *Come closer, closer*
Draws you to me like magnet
Fantasy, yet real
Let me soon devour delicious, ripe, so colorful
So warm and pleasingly ready
My composure soon disarmed
I feel so heady
Arms still outstretched, long
With inviting motion
*Come closer, come closer*

At the end of frozen, begging arm
Hands open facing heaven
Fleshy palms open
Reiterating *Come to me*
The lifelines on this palm
Distinct genetic mark
Echo the electrified, silent language of
*Come closer*

Arm, hand, now fingers
In artistic freeze join chorus
*Come closer*
Prominent the pointed middle finger
Shaped like the curved boat in your direction
In rocking motion *Come closer*

The pinky, index fingers join
All in hush silence asking for surrender
The index fingers motions
*Come closer*

Knowing that you are keenly aware
Of each and every juxtaposition
My hand in slow rhythm again motioning

*Come closer*

At last so close, the tender touch
By finer tip as Adam did touch Eve
The thrill, the victory, the bond
Whole hands do gently clasp
The bodies drawn, excited, yet restrained
Closer to each other joining in unity

## Action Theater

Action theater
What is that?
A stage full of action
Smell and sweat

Shoeless, barefoot stands intent in space
At first the actor stage discreet
I study body, arms, moving strange contorted face
Arms outstretched, body gyrating in motion
Movement contortion
Dramatic, steps still have no notion
A few sounds, facial expression
Rejecting to anger, fright
Acceptance and delight
The floor does seem to move
Actors act and must behoove
10 second story mimed, gesticulated sounds
Flaying hands and arms, bending, never ending
Emotion says come to me, come say hello
I block you away, now stay
No time for intimacy
Just exchanging charms
Tease and toss- hands, legs and shoulders
Well-lit ballet studio contains a face
Actor often retreat to walls
Often against the wall crucified or glued
In angst they seem pursued
Affront on the attack

In twos or fours
Communicate instantaneous
Special feeling knack, criss-cross and back
Nine and half shots in five minutes time
It is a stage, theater, past mime

For some full motion and expression
Audience and actor know, feel, guessing
Next moment's session
Sometimes a few staccato words
Hum or sound, chorus of giants
As long as movement
The body is around
Lie flat, ballet, glide
Movement, grace, grimace
Tone always open, cannot hide
Bird's song, angry expression
Painful moan

All joined, enmeshed, stretched
A spirit of erection
Unusual, universal
Theater of action

## *Life, Challenging Fun*

Where can we turn?
It's heaven or hell
I've been there
Know it well

Son, daughter, friend
Crisis? It's up to me and you
What *is* true happiness?
I don't have a clue

Life twisted, challenging fun
Onward, forward, upward, on the run
Mostly my choice, our selection
Rewards (good and bad) self satisfaction

Next time turn your life inside out
Change, challenge, effort
That's what our life is all about
Tears replaced by chucking laughter
Ring in frolic, festive after

It's not stewing
Life is doing
Tasty mixture of concocted sauce
It's your banner, it's your cause
Open eyed march join with glee
Jump the hurdles, solve the puzzle's secret key

Won some, lost some, but matured
Quizzical, curious new adventures lured
Young in mind, in heart and smart
Each new challenge your exiting start

Rejuvenate, reborn your only cost
Wage the future, win more, little lost
In spirit full of hope and zest
You're here, you're doing, you are blessed.


## Half Asleep

If you awake at twilight time
Half rested, groggy, half sublime
Dared in the netherworld
A grey, uncertain curtain now unfurled

Where am I to go
What to do          I do not know
Should I recline, eyes closed refrain
Say goodbye          off to sleep again

Half-baked, with great effort awake
Dare take the world on for the moment's sake
Laugh, cry or numbly observe
Until I strike my every titillating nerve

Split white into the rainbow colors burst
Touch up to the sky, nourish from the rippling brook
Savor the cool over lips, tongue still thirsts
Eat Adam's apple shamelessly until heaven strikes
Now with enthusiasm explore my many likes

Go to my friend, adore and kiss
Embrace hug with zest and bliss
Write, shape my dream, blend every ray
Roll out my carpet for my judgement day

'Twas now, 'twas here is ever present still
Awake I choose my path and tame my will
Share joy, infatuate the air with love
Active, a doer all around and from above

Tie the knot with deep humility and grace
Bruises about to heal and mend the human race
Though I be but a simple soul
I like you, am part of the human whole

Step up my dance, a tiny dot in vast universe
My active being causes waves to touch and then reverse
My heart in rhythm with your heart
Rejoicing in most challenging new start

The cycle of our day does end
We do adore, thankful as friend to friend
Observe the baby's cry to cheerless giggling laugh
That babe was you or I touched
By the magic staff

To grow and live
To take shape and give
Back to rest and sleep
For what our mind has trapped
Captured and retain to keep

Sleep now, to rejuvenate, repair and heal
In full command to act upon what I now feel
Watch out, my desire now more certain
On center stage fulfill my act before a full drawn curtain

### Head Start

He who laughs first
Has a head start
Can chuckle even after

### Never Find

We all gave the court a run for
Their money
Ours we could never find

## *You, In My World?*

It comes easy
Sometimes wheezy
To tell you
I love you
In rhyme

You mock me
Lost my prime
Aged wizard still
Over the hill

Cancel date communication
Not my feelings, a perplex situation
Not my longing, my urge
I'm still reeling closer, as my spirits will merge

Or will they?

One-sided, wanting to touch   to feel   to kiss
Wanting eyes, ears     your form I  miss

It's all in me, with me
        I step closer
        I look closer
        I breathe heavier
        I am closer

Adore your eyes
My feelings are real
Can you hear me
Can you see me
Can you feel me

I am in your world
Can't you be in mine

# The Jew

Ironic! The supposed effeminate Jew
The survivor no one knew
With bowed head seemed ashamed
Blemished, blamed
Some blond, some with a Semitic look
Large nose, tiny hook
Pedantic, cosmopolitan, inquisitive
Compassionate, charitable
One who can give
Music, theater and prayer
Artisan, healer, soothsayer

Once a cornered animal so clever
Brilliant repartee
Comic uses his humor as a lever
In the past, in his Staedle* most proud
Adhere to rigid Ghetto rules
Yet questions, hearty debate was allowed

Mingle, marry his own kind
Impregnate grandiose values into every Jewish mind

Though chased, tortured, almost enslaved
Men's evil enemy called *hate* he braved
Nobel Prize winners, scholars, scions of invention
To uplift mankind always his intention
Enlightened, now freed
Jews now part of our great world's creed
Each life so precious, still we all need a lift
Each human memory blessed
By that eternal, most spiritual gift

This creature, so eclectic from a people now reborn
Defies the world, in ignorance these Jews they did scorn
Selected to bring Torah treasures to this realm
Apostles to lead mankind at their helm

Call them Hebrews, call them Jews
These people of the book make news
Today, of no special race, place or face
Barely three generations before
Family, study, traditions they would most adore

Thus this new Jew, entrenched, more sure
For justice, understanding he will tour

*small village

54

Fighter, in the forefront for human rights
Protect young, old and sick, to every one's delight

Vigorously question all the world's values
Destroy the devil, goal is mankind's peace
Eternal peace in this world and the next
Try to follow the Torah and bible text

Destroy the devil, goal is mankind's peace
Eternal peace in this world and the next
Follow the Torah and the bible text
As King David long ago exclaimed
Uplift, help heal those too weak
Those who are still maimed

With love and work, a new beginning is so rife
So emulate and practice
As if all is part of our everlasting life

## I Do What I Can

He said
I am an old man
I do what I can
I cannot change the sky and sea
They are open, blue
I join and celebrate our Jubilee
What I have saved and what I earn
Infinitesimal you will leave
I fall ill
In my will
Many will benefit
With that distinction I'll get rid
Still I am an old man
I do what I can

## *Evaporate*

The rapids tested

The silver torrent cascades between the

      steep and narrow boulder

Now water     slowly     spreads over

      a slivery  glistening lake

The boat steers placid, easy to maneuver

Heading majestically down stream

      to meet the wide, inviting open-aired

      lake

Only to evaporate, rekindle

      With steaming grace


## *The Carnival*

At the carnival,
A charade of men and women
All shapes and forms
Slim  tall  fat   big bosomed
Hairy   bald   weird

Common denominator
Human species
In a carnival celebration

Cheap, abundant food and drink
A space, a seat for a price
Dressed in pants or shorts
Two ears
Inquisitive participation
Two eyes
So squeal
Exit human

I never said they were good or bad
Who am I to judge
All I said was that they are human beings

## Fled The Nest

The tragedy of love and bliss
Is when the mother bird
Gives infant the last bite
After painful birth

Must let it fly on its own
To try
At its own discretion
Once image and reflection
Own creation now finds a new direction

So you and I have left the nest
Some time ago swam towards new shores
Yet wind and sail against the elements obsessed
Sometimes the less we rudder in the boat
While nature does the rest
We look on, steer
Some of us go under... disappear

It is a voyage
Each so different

Fraught with danger and events

Love, desire and recants
Involved, delirious
We follow aspiration serious
Nothing but the best

In our zeal, our work so heavily obsessed
For most it's one trip and no more
End at heaven's gate and shore
Can delay, but not return
We've grown up, always to learn
As aged the trip must end
Our fire dimmed
We do return
To dirt and sound
Despite a final battle, fight
To bring us on the voyage
Never to return

Our struggle, destiny and flight
Cannot flee the eyes of heaven and hell

Through eyes which on us constantly dwell
The truth of our inner life revealed
Our hopes and dreams in death are so concealed

Get off the boat
Steer, new shore, different course
Arrive or not, have no remorse
For if you failed
Be proud, saw much

You sailed


## No Money, Who?


So many billionaires
Working so hard to preserve
Enlarge their enterprise and empire
Strip them of wealth and power
Who truly are they?

## Let The World In

Open the window
Let the world in
Share      inhale
See the moon light beams
Craters, shadows in your eyes

Hear rustling leaves, walls of grey
Out in space things are not always what they seem
New sounds and smells without delay

Cold air, warm air fresh and awake
Hustle and bustle
Gather your things, your soul
Leave, get out for goodness sake

What if it rains?
What if snow comes inside?
What if grey dust permeates the air?
Just close the window
Let sound and world bounce off the window pane

## Better Something (Fill-In)

Stop. Guilt. Do you _____
It's about_____
She never_____ I like_____
Every time I make a mistake_____

Better something than_____
It's all_____
Why didn't you_____?

I _____
Give me some good_____

# *Doors*

I.

Doors in our life
The opportunities
Of yesterday
From labor hospital room
To crib at home
Our first security
From room to room
The classroom door so tall
With anxious faces waiting for the bell
First hotel room
Down the hall
Her bed most prominent of all
Beyond each door a dear one
Parent, siblings
Finally the lover
How secretive
How secure
Our room, to kiss to hug
Massage and rub
Do the things that lovers do
Greeting doors
Rejecting doors
Doors simply man's tools
Tall doors for the brilliant and the fool

Older doors to interviews
Doors of sadness, gladness and good bye
Through door
Comes the view

I am sitting in my bedroom
Door wide open
Messiah and hopeful friends
Never an intruder
The free open door delight
Away from multitude of strife
Prophets Armageddon

Some have a lock
Some many locks
Some doors inviting
Some exciting

Some squeak
Some tilted

II.

Imagine yourself
Which doors have you entered
Ah so many each day
Today, conscious

From space to space
In the privacy of our study
The bathroom, basement and attic
Doors that hold secrets

Many doors of lifetime
Box in the spacious room
Dazzling view beyond
Which novels did I enter
Doors show the disarray of its inhabitant
Pain and helpless nerves of abysmal poverty

The door automatic to the elevator
Open in hotel
The heavy, unencumbered door into the building
Rushing to make the bus before the door closes
So many, many open doors
Taking me to curious
Destinations

Doors of many colors
Great hopes
Doors of fear, frustration
Doors I never want to enter again
Doors once opened
See those human angelic faces
Part of youth
Parents young, bidding
Full of love, endearing

Exciting doors into theaters
Concerts
Ballet
Most splendid choruses

III.

Which doors will I open tomorrow

Will I perceive man's war at first glance

Doors where reception celebration
Overwhelms me

Yes there were doors slammed in my face
Doors closed, finger caught
Shoulder banged, bleeding nose

Doors are solid, demanding
Swinging

It all depends if you enter or leave

Doors are merely extensions of
Our boxes that we live in
Doors of separation, of sound
Of smell, of life

If you play with pet birds
Never leave doors open
(I am your pet bird)
For truly doors are not natural
Where in the mountain, valleys
Expansive open meadow field
Do you see doors?

## *Start Fresh*

give me a gift
      give me a life
            give me escape
                  from form, from shape


                meticulous     start fresh


                let my best parts in symmetry mesh

    remade to challenge all

my future happiness I call

## Sweater

I thank the beast
Whose hair I wear and feast
It's hugging, covering my upper frame
I understand the sheep so shorn
Will never be the same
Until new growth of hair
Its nakedness repair

Alpaca wool, cashmere
Plain or fancy design knit
When it's chilly cold
I hold this sweater dear

So thank you shearer, knitter
With this gorgeous sweater
In all the comfort
I feel fitter


## Cold Season

Canadian ice cold wind
Crashes down upon the vast, rich landscape
Freezing, dusty white coat
Punishing as if we really sinned
Decorating leaves, pines
In magic noble shape

Alas the cold freeze kills
Nature downcast waits for thawing spring
White flakes waft down upon G'd's will
Wrap everything in blanket of pure white

Chill wind and ice
A testimony to a power beyond reach
The azure sky, sparkling stars surmise
All below, respect it seems to teach

Some fog in skating or observe the ice dance
Ice fish or hunting, photograph a picturesque
White-grey winter scene,
Chilly brisk wind
Most of us stay inside

Hibernate with book, TV, computer
Outside too cold to change
From distance watch cool landscape most serene

We wait for the thaw of spring
Longer, sunnier days
We hear the sound whistle of the water music ring
Read about the freeze, the traffic and delays

Icicles, once smoking breath
Defy the elements so stern
Knowing full well this season sounds
A white and cold and deathly ring

I remember you dear friend and kiss
Huddled, heavily garbed, may all rest in peace
Your spirit everywhere so happy and jolly
Your time did come in this mostly unfriendly season
Even cemeteries are desolate, grey, isolated
Waiting for a warmer day


## What If?

What if...
A stroke, diminished walk
Crippled , immobile yet I talk
While brain alert and keen
So desperate to rule, command
As for a lifetime it had been
Free thought to act

That free mind's craving and desire
Do body's bidding, never tire
So in the act the joust, laugh and joy
Each new devilish adventure a new game or toy
With chess like moves against men and nature
Enjoy the rhapsody and mortal pleasure
Grateful to partake, thankful for each measure
Mind cogent, planning does perceive
Calculate, compute the echo of each feeling
With soul wrenching deep belief
Excitement of the joy of life, my own fief
Until with sneaky stealth and terrifying power
Doctor confirms disintegration at this hour
I fear
I need, I must keep long lived freedom
The free spirit chained within is still alive,

Tortured prisoner, in tortured body
Cut, maimed with a bloodless knife

What if... helplessness, paralysis set in
What if... the answer scares me as I move my pen


## I Love You

I love you Lillian Weil
Grand beauty, in fashionable style
Conservative, dignified
Mother, adviser
Ability to explain, digest, to synthesize
Quietly so proud
Never complain, greatly admired, never loud

Potent, disarming, always charming voice
Message wise and profound
The listener marvels, given choice
Didactic, compromiser, persuasive, direct
Honest, able wise pearls with taste and tact
Situation most exact, gifted to lead
Wonderful being, voice and deed

Servant, open hearted, nice
Willing, no money, salary or price
My wife and lover for 44 years
The last few weeks so hard and full of tears

So incredibly sad
What joy and pain
When will I see you Lillian once again?


## Decide, Awake

They say it is not wise
To make momentous decisions
While you are half asleep
So why not wake and run away
Let fate, faith and destiny cram your style!

# Do What's Right

Nothing is sacred, everything is sacred
Will I be upright, truthful, a liar faking it?
Society through parent's heritage in youth
Determines right and wrong, ultimate truth

The dandelion and the poppy flowers
Sway like a rolling sea in unison with powers
The song of nightingale or starling so unique
Marvel like child. The need to touch, taste and seek

I feel my way through puzzled paths
Seeking to accept the predestined master's wrath
Indestructible like a child ever testing the truth
Abhor, reject the evil uncouth

I have taken what's not mine, it's true
Conjured, covered up, lied till my face turned blue
Fictitious deeds, accolades never earned
Cheated, betrayed thereby much friendship spurned

With maturity the concessionaire sorted right from wrong
Sometimes in silence or loud burst, always a truthful song
The laws of G'd and nature should keep me in check
I do amend my errors, try hard to compensate for what I do lack

Turn the cheek with humility, help the old and sick
Fight temptation, my bastion one of honesty, from mortar and brick
I err, I lie, deceive
Not deliberately or with intent
I tread a crooked cursed road
In tournament the devil's side I honor and defend

I do not walk on lofty air or water
Cherish life, man's son and daughter
So back to work, to meditate or play
Knowing each day is judgement day

The scale awaits
Can we weigh opinion, thought
Our Western culture ever changes
Our value system modified and often bought

So with firm conviction
Stay the course
Do what I know and think is right
The truth, firm in concrete
If in doubt the devil fight
Take your God-given seat

It's then known
Uphold the teaching of parents and children
Despite temptation and the carrot stick

Refuse evil decisions, follow G'd's right

## *Idiotic Cage*

The mesh at the locked door
Stern male nurses evermore
Of course I'm not demented
Insane, outcast, deeply resented
I simply stare through the patches
Of the barred window
Hemmed in like a delirious animal
About to pounce in another escape
It is I who should shout crime or rape
As I remember a lightning rod aimed
Time distant, medication brain impregnated
Alert, not violent, not sedated
Of the brave new world
Smoothly and obliquely
Deterred

Gene replacement, body implants
Supersonic travel, my queer mind so demented
Computer stations, thought controls
Glide, hand-held robot handled now routine
Pull strings from secret abode, secret screen

Superhuman, superman, super ceded
Predictable programmed, how much needed
How far are man's expansions
Crazy, like me reverts and pushes buttons

Oral commands, post-hypnotic commands
Make the impossible possible, transform
Another generation from the norm
So you see, they say I am crazy

Every day, in every way
Machines computers - our servants
Or we are servants of them
As we slave long arduous hours
There are celebrations and there are scars
While belittle and show never behind these bars

I, who hallucinate, crazy clown
With me I rate
Irrational, extreme, blasphemous
I've long landed from the moon
On a strip of light beams on a canyon cushion
Orgies of a most impossible world
Ignited by secret demons
Ready to destroy a secret world
A lifetime of building
A moment to destroy society
Shucks, the lady guards, patiently will
Live where you are not

Help – I painfully beg through the bars
Help an idiotic sinner
Return to reason
Sparkling hope, future
Lived in Nirvana, coming to collect
Growing immense – need space
Hack   toil   create
Awkwardly yet full of grace
Eat any meal so blinded by the ads

Future plans, spin, spin
Blindly follow fads,
Special friends, special collection
Love – work       hypnotic
Work mixed with drive and pleasure
Thoughts of accompaniment, so grandiose

Guard or matron or copper
Whoever you are
Reward me, touch me, guess what's next
Free me – pressure cooker of too much
Better let me hallucinate
Hold my hand in friendship or despair

Space ship on earth, so full of grace
Let me out of here before I loose my real sanity
Then, after all you are the outside prisoner
Looking complex at me


## *Topple The King*


At the pinnacle of control
Bring 'em down! The new confrontational goal!
Bring me down and I'll kill!
Let's knock that king off the hill!


Our competitive nature says go, be a *getter*
Surpass competition, exert to be better
Using clever knowledge      devious means to surpass
Goal to succeed, to be first in the class


Yet we trample over ruins to get to the top
Competitors at the way side, ignored and don't stop
Defeated, enemies are left behind
Our balanced, jovial personality now crass, so unkind


Call it success, winning the part
Lonely on top, the battle won hard
In this aspiring contest full of guts and nerve
Can we retain human conscience, get what we deserve?


Can we still be grateful, a bit humble?
Or rough wielding giants lost in a jungle
Can we balance, re-appraise
A touch of human kindness and grace


Foolish victors thinking they can win every race
Of course not! Restore a touch of compassion and grace
Maybe see the blessing in humankind
Open eyes and heart      show we're not blind


Do we have to lose a bit of our soul
To heal, make ourselves whole?
Hope, coupled with determination pays
Can we dare return to society with a new, mature and wiser face?

## Wringing Out The Mind

when we wring out the mind

always another
        drop            of wisdom


        slowdown
        patience

be honest                with thyself

        the orange
            FULLY squeeeezed

                                    The towel stopped
                d
                  r
                    i
                        p
                        p
                            i
                            n
                              g

the mind says
            make this a healthy delicious me


            the mind says
                        help

    really means it

                    deny the mind/follow the mind

## Love's Invitation

Alone in my huge house
To meander and carouse
She rejected my invitation
So my love is cooled, not yet our separation

Why don't you stay?
No harm, no fray
I love a warm body
Everyday

Nice to awaken
God forsaken
With another head near-by
Glance admirably, heavenly sigh

A luscious kiss hello
Know every touch is warm and real
Know that it's so
For the moment, I never want to go

## Ride Of Life

Prophetic gestures
Words based on longevity
3 score plus 10
Ideas, stories for children, for the birds
Why not listen once again?

G'd made the world in six days
Rested on the seventh
A perfect world
For Man to spoil
So heaven would recoil.

A world now upside down to fix
G'd, please redo the days from one to six.
Mostly seven
Does your man child not deserve some heaven?

Want equality for all
Each person on his merit does his share
Opportunity, each of us different – so unfair
Compassion for the children, old,    we care

All this so trite
You and I know something is not right

Humanity so full of freedom and choice
Society to interchange without restraint
Moderate decimals of tolerance, not noise
An honor system with no guilt where no one will be blamed

Alas, from birth on, no two of us alike
Each human nurtures, raised so different
Each of temperament and psyche
Each from two strains, leaving a different scent

If the world reborn
All equal on the day of birth
Each one of us would take a different tour
Size up the universe with glee and mirth

Within days, all be unequal once again
Each in a contest for his shadow, his place
The brilliant strong, their voice and weight would soon sustain
Woe to new wars, new conflicts of the human race
Yes, doors of opportunity for all
If you have brains and motivation
Dare try your luck, overcome the fall
The futile wait, go venture to your private station

The ride of life unfair
Fraught with excitement, danger and despair
Gigantic trip, adventure of a lifetime long
On its way accompanied by love's most
Charming mesmerizing song

Yours to heed
Yours to keep

## Knows Too Much

He who knows too much
Is overwhelmed with facts and such
Can not discern his soul from earth
Knows what his empathy is truly worth
He's always right
Yet the intangible slips from sight
Emotion of the high and low
His is the star, the epitome, the show

Flesh on flesh
He'll soon succumb and mesh
With plebian underlings     innocent
Unable to communicate
He must escape    return to throne
Pontificate     demonstrate his facts
Be it robot       computer driven brain
The shower of his fact list embraces in vain
Great pain to know too much
Hold back in disdain
Reiterate the human touch
Of patience   kindness    deep affection
Go meet your own, dissect your satisfaction

## Narcissus Celebration

I capture my own rapture
Narcissus wings I swoon
Enveloped in perfume of love
A slave I sing my courting tune

Is it the tired reproducing hormones
Sending their message to the brain
Like an anvil drives the demon sex
Takes his swollen turn, explodes     not to be seen again

Advent of age, last celebration
Energy reduced, full of elation
The crave for touch, love, kisses
Endearment, adoration never misses

Under cover, innocent
Delirious, delectable we do depend
A twosome     we satisfy our hunger much younger

Unending appetite
No questioning is it *right*?

Delight
The rapture that I capture

## *Feelings O.K.*

Feelings are neither right or wrong
Yours, mine    they are there
If you sing a happy or sad song
Your internal story ceases a heroic dare

If the other party cannot see
It's I who feels, it's really me
You advise: *Stop feeling. It's really not that bad.*
You don't understand, are you a bully or a cad?

I feel for you with deep emotion
To you I am a figure full of motion
My longing and desire
To be with you, to share and never tire

You have other interests and friends
You have your own feelings to make amends
You have your world isolated from mine
A pain, a wounded hole within, a longing sign

To feel, admit longing is no sin
Unless irrational, overwhelming, desperate
Yet I think of you as lover more than kin
I feel for that and this – embrace beyond the kiss

I know there is more to life
A stable full of friendship will suffice
Just for now the empty, forlorn feeling is still there
It isn't easy, rejection coupled with loneliness is hard to bear

Our day with time an ever turning wheel
The meter, scale so personal I feel
But that is life
I, like all lovers, will survive

## Day's End

          end
     fatigue of day


          our mind                    so tired
                                                      goes astray

today
               a good time

                         all in
                         swill and prime
conversation is just

          employee did the rest


                         the food permissive
                         time flashed
                         clean up sporadic


                                   (don't remind me of the attic)

stock market


                    dive


stocks jumpy                              alive

it's hard to complain

               think of touch, of love again

          think of today's happenings

wrenching pain

bad again   almost fatal (but not)

tomorrow we celebrate

## *Late Night Junkies*

I am an aberration
A mirror of a queer sensation
Addicted
Depicted as a TV Junkie
Only....
I am lonely
So silently content
To spend
Wasteful hours
Watching ghastly news
As all about me sours,

Introspective   predictable   vicarious
A time, life eating monster screen
The droning, mesmerizing sound
Echoes into the dullness of my junkie brain
Seven thousand killed in earthquake
Polished politicians promise
Give me a break
Grizzly murder, stocks gyrate
Poison, knife, gun, rape and get away
Hammers on the news anvil
With angle shots at night or day
Cartoons, commercials intersperse
Open mouthed, entranced, enhance
Make it worse
Now the gangster, detective film grunts on
The dawn does beckon
My hulk, demented mind and body reckon
Some rest, some sleep, no more escape
Must tear away from deadly, dopey magnet called TV
Must get some sleep, must break the chain
Once again be free
A terrible affliction, destroying coy addiction
A punishment, a beating

The night is gone
Will daylight too be fleeting

Do dare I soon awake
Curse the devils doing as I take
This next day I rue
Fatigued, exhausted I feel blue
Stupidity its own price
The tragic punishment a lesson and advice
What glues us to the tube
Is it curiosity, intellect
Personal entertainment we are seeking?


## Miss You

I too like you have lost
A relative, a friend to mourn
Ingrained in a vivid memory
I close my eyes, almost touch
Though dead sojourn

I see your smile, your sadness close
Remember love, touch and such
I hurt, your apparition shows
In silence your ghost steals the part
Within my mind distinct
Vision now is mine to keep at last
I see your piercing eyes, your textured skin
I hear your voice, you're here, you're in
Love, friend dear, dear departed
From early age you were with me
You never parted, I feel you close
Your smile, your ears, your nose
As I laugh and cry worlds apart
Pain and joy within tissues of my heart
I knew you then
I know you now

I'll treasure you forever inside my grey cells
Behind my brow

Yet we must live a steadfast, fruitful life
Regain composure, strength as we survive
Celebrate those lost just now
One life to live, to give
Adversity somehow
Still drown with many tears but no regrets
Meet soon in faith I build
A better world with you instead

## *Do My Thing*

Top of mountain charm, fertile deep below
Life in extremes, euphoria next to despair
Dawn and dusk in the eerie afterglow
My human want, my drive to care

From youth to ebb of life
I, learn to love/hate
I will enjoy partake, survive
Thankful of each precious meal on every plate

The brain schemes and directs
I stand erect, follow duty, obligation plan
I wonder, ponder, thoughts I will dissect
Eager, blind enthusiasm
Do the best I can

Late at night, accomplished, eyelids
just about to close
Add up kaleidoscopes of yesterday
The morrow brings new zest
Adversarial thought, negative I must dispose
Balance duty, sport, meal and play
Make tomorrow better than today

We human creatures stirred by feeling most
profound
Born with a yell, in silence dig eternal rest
Through life we bustle with a fury and loud sound
We build and lose, challenge all
in readiness of every test

Briskly I do my thing, sing my tune
Rotate creative between sun up and moon
Convinced there's much wonder still ahead
I have so little time in life, as years fly by
Know what I make, do sow
I will beget

Inspired with hope, with dignity
Steer toward happiness
Until I too will die
But not until ....

## You Are Not G'd

After a long rest
Giant man is free
Chain untied
World ready, right
There is a storm about to brew
Man's joy of life, of love
Now rejuvenated new
About to consume and succeed
Unfathomable strength, impossible feat
Creative genius nurtured with amazing zest
The world so infinite, starting yet grotesque
In arrogance I want to rectify
O put my earthen stamps
Move the mountain
Change the world

Huge colossus, your turn to shoot
Victory now or abort
Yet one bit of advice
I'll say it thrice

You are not G'd
You are not G'd
You are not G'd


## Nature's Way

The storm excites, brings oceans to a boil
Torrents drench, soak spill over all and soil
Thunder, earth reverberates and mountains shake
Destroying nature, man-made toil
Overwhelms all rhyme and reason without
for goodness sake
Nature's way to level give and take

Impossible to stop rotation of our earth
With climate changes, tides, floods and fire
No matter what all mankind and globe are worth
The crust of mountain, oceans
earth we damn and do admire

Immense contortions of gigantic proportion our surprise
Nature, so omnipotent thrashes according

to its own demise

Our system, blood and brain
Vicissitudes of life sustain
When calm will soon return
The stormy elements subside
We humans in an austere planet year
Thankful for survival
after nature's boisterous ride

Never ready for the next onslaught
So as the day and night, nature turns and twists
Where hell and hang men often caught
Awaking us from our midst

With each new end, a new
beginning will ensue
Growth and ripeness harvest rich
Earthling reform, proclaim there is
a G'd so true
Soon proclaim the Golden Calf's fall
into the devil's niche

Until a new pox, pestilence and nature
thunder does proclaim
Self-propagating life is fleeting, a precious gift
Beware, do dare that endless game
Let me survive, be there tomorrow
for I have long lived

## Bedtime

Bedtime, I couldn't sleep
Turned off the music and TV
Shut the window
Lights out again
Unplugged the phone
Then in utter silence
Found my busy imagination
In outer space, raising Cain
So creatively busy in fact
I couldn't go to sleep

Romantic feelings, sensual visions
Conjure the touch and taste of romance's norms
Passionate love of past, when to revive
Penned down on the mattress, hormones dance alive

Partnership like friendship intertwined
Though often lovingly and kind
Always the danger of too much intimacy
Divergent views discussed, feelings despite tolerance
The appetite of the intellect duels to explain
Easy first meeting next frivolous relationship
Coupled with friendship into test of partnership
Glued, good intentions
Each in his own world tolerant, ready to compromise
Confront major decisions and we realize
It's hard to part, much harder to dissolve


The ice-cold pain and agony, divorce so imminent
It's our feelings and our value system we cannot recant
Subvert controlled by dominance, persuasive friend
No matter what      who doesn't understand
Unlike a chameleon, my mold of values now so strong
I realize we can't compromise and don't belong
Together


My chest and feelings hurt, I cry
Cannot go back to sleep
You understand and now know why


## *Control*


In youth and older age we play with lives
Awed, loved, teased –but not with other's wives
Manipulate, cajole, threaten, place guilt
Punish and reward until our ego filled

It starts with parents and their kids,
Intelligent and brawny pushing in our midst,
Do this, do that – a tenuous, scary cry
The receiver awed and he knows why

Once educated by the life of deed and school
Ingrained  controlling values now use this tool
Do this, do that – the lackey servant paid
Silently or quite direct we order unafraid

As we dominate and conjugate into old age
We mellow, still dictate the innocent old sage
The tide does turn and twist
Infirm and weak, still served our wishes now dismissed

So with our brawny brains new empires we build
It's always on other's shoulders the orders often filled
I guess from birth, man's designated training is to control
He does it often, devious and open, an expensive heavy toll

You too are on the pecking order
Your turn long gone just look around the border
Go mellow, with sensitivity treat your companion with compassion
For you may be manipulated and treated in same fashion

*Puzzle*

Out of                    desperation
We grab

          LIFE   by a

                      hair

a hopeful sensation
        rescue from despair

If we but solve the
p   u   z   z   l        e

how we feel

                 (why)

     we see the absurdity

          soon appeal
coupled with action

      dig out
      of this
      morose

                    situation

                                        recognize the aberration
        Touch
                    possibilities of

            success

    if we do or                                        don't
                                            it's a lot more stress

Sourness contaminates our search for happiness


## *Words Analyzed*

Words tied together
Like a chain mysteriously
Analyzed, acknowledged
By the electric train
Out in now
Do don't why
Significant
I should live so long


## *Tell*

Hidden fear, touch of fright laziness
Dare freeze
Not productive
Dare tell all
Tell some
Or tell
The lucky would
Will never know

# Innocence of Youth

Alert, enthralled jump into action
Young person meets the challenge great
Like a festive meal piled on the world, that is your fate
Mesmerized    pure    sheer    strong will
Conquer wrong, dissatisfaction grinding in the value mill

I choose, I choose
Youngster certainly surmises
New manipulation twists
Most shocking, bottom line surprises

The whales, the frogs, the trees
The poison seeping deep beyond our knees
Milk-fed ducks, precious fur from mink and fox
Carcinogens pollute earth water, a most killing pox

Then there are man's arrogant, stupid wars
There's cancer, heart disease, as HIV infections soar
Man combatant of man, man steals from man
Abhorrent, millions incarcerated in the can

Oh young one, your wingspread soaring with delight
World's landscape to be tilled so wide
Nourish, till and sweat at harvest time
Harvest of healing, of compassion in this rhyme

Revolt, redraw what is really true
Change nature, man into a golden glue
Of fairness, justice through new vision to survive
Harness the hate, religious strife, new vision to new life

Oh you blue, black, brown green eyed hope

So young and innocent blood boiling
With man's other, optimum world elope
Discard the weeds, spread the seeds

We, older generation wise
Still obstacle and brake of newness on the rise
Where would life's values change
Were it not for newborn babe, new world so bright and strange

To get there – give up time and sacrifice
Maybe, just maybe someday
Collect the golden magic of surprise

## Victory In Defeat

He, who in defeat can muster, stand most erect
For him or her I bow with deep respect
He who dares with vengeance to get even in contempt
The challenge is to stay away from such anger pent
You loser, you hater, there's a life of challenge far ahead
Keep your venom far away from me, a pricey toll
Clear out your head, regroup the mind and muscle now instead
It's good to lose at times, appreciate the whole
It's healing love that nourishes my soul

You know the miserable loser never did appear
Saber's sharp for battle, that's why I am now here

Sometimes it's hard to acknowledge our world
It's here, it's all you have, in front of you a pearl
Green fields, deep valleys so admiring
Lost in the canyon streets so awe inspiring
Return in spirit, see your zest of youth
Break nasty habits away from home and narrow booth

It's participation, give it all your best
So if you win or lose      you did it as an earthy  guest
The fun and joy advent of new game you will master
Go play participate, the dice rolling ever faster

# *Delirious Feelings*

There is a drive to excess
     Not express
Feelings, alive    real
Feelings inside    throbbing I feel
Anxious  hopeful  better tomorrow
Life longer    time I can borrow

Sight of old friend, spark of love
Voice sweet    dear, song of the dove
Banners of touch    friendship appear
Security   health  infinite wealth
Mine to hold    secure my abode

Delirious   happy   touch of heaven on earth
Long life lived    memories well worth
Touch, tongue    care  dare
Who has time?   Enticing  to share

I'm overflowing
It's all there

Rhythmic romantic scenes reappear
Lover's emotion transmitted to each tear
How heavenly comes through vision and sound
We feel it everywhere   wall   chandelier  all around

Love  hate  denial  rejection
All part of counterpoint   now deep projection
Music now smooth, toned down    exact
Lovers vow dangerously   blindly enter the pact

Ah, the jealous other suitor with desire
Stalks, schemes    will reap their ire
Out to destroy the lovers with deadly fire
He lays the trap
Slips, falls    no strength    poor sap
Fumes   acid   gas devours
They miraculously escape that very hour

Truth and honor unfurled
Lovers enter the all embracing world
So lucky, together, abundant choice
Escaped to their chamber like little girls and boys

## Just One More Exercise

Just one more exercise
The athlete will excel
Twice the prize
Poet uninspired
Will he abandon his craft or be retired?

No. Determination, concentration
Self-fulfilling goal will have own approbation
Word painting full of action
The canvas full, so deadly vivid- no retraction

To contemplate, dreams into words, a burning lark
Storage of wisdom into the printed word
Behind author's mask
Each sentence, paragraph glued to the next
The author's mind pours on the livid text

Though truth and fiction often mixed
Ingrained on paper fluid ideas now fixed
While readers reinterpret, reinvent the word
Most tales are long, while others short and dead

The world gobbles up these most delicious books
On every topic that the author cooks
Like mitosis, the stories do spread
As if a spirit, soul on and transfer now well read

Know that the writer's influence is far beyond his being
The world now close, word pictures millions one now seeing
The word incisive, festers far exceeds the power of the sword
Telegraphed, digested into deed does plead next action

Inspired, almost religious invitation to write and describe
The word spread and planted soon to ripe
A touch of G'd, that only humans understand
Nature's omniscient power, all of us in awe
Few understand

So free-flow I shall write into the night and court
The writing vehicle so telling with deep import
Spout forth the senseless of world's right and wrong
From music, movement to brawny building is my song

## I Loved Her

I loved her once
Thought I did
Enamored, charmed like a teenage kid
I loved her figure, her soft, sexy voice
I loved her thoughts further transcending my choice
I loved her hips, her shapely legs
I loved pure beauty, all her sex
I dreamt her vision morn and night
I dream it frequent burning bright
I yearned for her touch, more and such
I wanted part of her to touch
I tasted love's thunder and my body burned
My mind seeing her I yearned
I felt in awe, melted when she talked and teased me
I knew she could and maybe would please me
Admirably in an unforgettable moment we kissed
Pent up emotion, what a heavenly foreboding twist

Then disaster, her treatment was full rejection
Somehow fickle folly, I was never part of her election

At times I think I still see her, now distant, full of glee
An ever melting, evaporating vision I can and could not see
So beautiful, so flawless, her body ingrained in my mind
An ecstasy, an apparition of the past, no more to find
Yet on occasion she now reappears
To test my taste, to haunt, re-awakening my tears
A fleeting time yet I did love her, most adore
She who has vanished and now is no more, no more

## Can't Sleep

4 am a window rattled, I awoke
It broke my dream, my sleep, no joke
I tried to fall asleep again
To no avail I lay inane

Conjured days duties in which I thrive
The errands, meetings to survive
The market, employees prepare for my trip
My stomach heavy, words on lips

In the deadly dark silence of the morn
My eyes hum awake, alive now reborn

So much to do yet tired
I yawn, lights on, sit up inspired
A snack, a TV show, a book
I'm overwhelmed by duty everywhere I look

Now 4:30 am, better take some sleeping pills
A furtive mind inactive, ever cures all mental ills
My day will wait
A busy day of good and bad my fate

So crawl, more tired under cover
Conjure, think of touch, kiss of lover
No, better count a thousand sheep
So mind at peace and back to sleep

My thumping heart in rhythm now relaxed
The body's mental system taxed
I, one of billions, eager and alive
Await the day to work and love to survive

The pills' effect, my eyelids close
A lonely quiet sleep, more daydream color ember
A song we each compose
In silence, honestly I do not remember


## I Am What You See

Innocent when born
Genes and mutations depict nature's choice and scorn
Dependent, free spirit to explore
A tiny ambulate that I adore
Perfect and imperfect to the core

Malefactor showers guilt and shame
Restrain and teach, try to tame
Question morality, reevaluate history
Explain unknown, deflate the mystery

Stored in the tentacles of brain
Reaction merged in feelings that do drain
Some higher I.Q., some brainy
Some free spirit erratic, bordering insanity

Yet each with gift to see, to feel, to touch
With pathos, empathy I see and love you very much
My body, brains and being
Are real, are true – it's what you're seeing

We do test, detest
Why not experiment challenge, do our best?
Free spirit to taste, to touch
Exult in love, ripe and overdo so much

To run away and run to whenever follows suit
To mix with world's forbidden fruit

Intoxicated, hypnotized and overrated
The blemished though pursues us unabated
Until observed, caught
Accusation, a feeling of guilt throughout

Reluctantly must now retreat
Avoid the censure, punishment
Grabbing the judge's seat
Admit the guilt, the folly of the game
Slightly mocked, revived
Plan a more structured life, more tame

I hope free spirit
Do unchain me yet from time to time
Let me retrieve the ghosts of
Friends and family of yesteryear

Share my reflection, introspection

So mellow
This clipped bird

## Too Busy

The religious man is
Weighed down by codes, tradition, laws
Therefore has less time and thought
To get into the worst trouble

## *Real or Fantasy?*

You are so lovely, beautiful, slender
I thrill to envision your sexy strident step
Love of life, of lips, of flesh defends
Of tantalizing touch, I nature's rep

Grateful, fantastic we share
Our bodies gently press, more anxious lips
I gorge and love each part of you and dare
I close my eyes, you my companion on a
thousand trips

Infatuation, too good to be true
How can this thrill and feeling last
I adore you if only you knew
Come close, come join, continue our blast

So thank your omnipotent one above
I cherish her, I idolize
I am in
Love

Are the medicines and hormones
Dancing their hallucinated act
I love it, I like it
That's a matter in fact

What else matters?

## *Revolution*

Every revolution breeds ideas
Embellished by the agitated masses
While the old regime, belatedly, feel like asses
The nerve, don't they deserve
Justice? Better times, perception
New commitment, products
False carrot, blithe promises, over confidence

The masses are
Not asses

Assure us of future care or
We'll throw the next rascals out
On a whim, let them pout
In essence we are told
Do more for the young and old
Care for the sick
Protect us from all enemies
From without and within
Let us rise each morning with determination
Avoid fear, poverty, and unnecessary death
Avoid the over indulgence, but celebrate a rational feast

So restructure the old institutions
Yet retain freedom of the mind, of expression
Experiment as long as your neighbors will not suffer
Communicate, disseminate newfound ideas
The people yes! The guided masses maybe. The oligarchy which
Has the one and only solution –NO!
Is it possible to have bloodless revolution or must
Blood be shed later?
We can always ignore, crawl under the cover
For how long? Don't we all need oxygen?

Remember, each revolution devours its own children
The price and prize is mankind's future
Need we rebuild what we have already built?


## *The Nerd*

A nerd does stupid things
Goes to bed at 2 am
Eats all day
Showers each person with words of jest and foolishness
Always pass the Nerdie test

Dresses like a nerd
Eats like a nerd
Sleeps like a nerd
Dances...
Always most absurd

Most of all nerds dream
Spacey, starry, weird
You know the kind
Never made the baseball team
Early rejected, merry, not unclean
At 28 mom still catered to a nerd
Most absurd

One day a maiden gorgeous, fair
Said to our nerd, *For you I care*

Within days of his new romance
After a delicious kiss and dance
*For you dear maiden I'll sacrifice*
*I'll buy new clothes*
*Learn manners to be nice*

In short, too bad
Our nerd went straight
Now he's like the others
Testing fate
Engaged, marriage in fume
Will we ever hear his familiar
Lopsided tune

Thank God the world is big enough
For Nerds and me
Without perspective
Where would I then be?

# Old Love... Teary Pearls

Fight with best friend
Ugly, direct, defend
Below the belt
Old wounds, openly felt

Anger      frustration
Epitaph showered, beyond ration
You lied    betrayed
Repartee, curse screeched out, unafraid

Why so direct, so callous and so crude
More low blows, insidious pain to boot
This is or was your friend
Fond lover, don't you understand

Hurt, tears, how could we
Why closest friend would we
Leave, shut up,      before it's too late
Precious friendship soon dissolved into a shambling state

Time, talk and meeting minds will heal
The piercing words
The scars we'll always feel
Some visible, some in the soul, all real

New love, new bond, new friendship will appear
Different, joyous, bold and dear
Embrace for each love different, intense
Soaks our emotion, mind immense

Old love, a trail of teary pearls now scattered
Replaced, nurtured since all love has mattered
This latest love so special and unique
We taste and toast our coitus as it reached its peak

# Knowing

Little did they know
That I knew
Not knowing I
Wasn't supposed to know
So now you know

## Stranger To Friend

first phrase

look into
    opponent's FACE

begins the   r   a   c   e

    of contact

flash            exchange

intellect          range

    It may be normal (strange)
    If the person, pleasant   nice

it's easy to  talk          break the ice

    if he's a contraire

you will defend
    rationalize and compare

         good luck

when next stranger becomes

    your friend

never know how long

    friendship lasts or

ends

# Rain

It's 12:37 A.M.
Gust, sheets of torrential rain
Incessant     loud     thrashing wet
Continuous, light drumming sound
Proud     most defying
Never dying

Everywhere, pools of soggy wet
The rows of silvery pearls bounce on their target
Receptive leaves deliver the cool liquid like teaspoon medicine gone wrong
Drip-drop unto the ground
A distant thunder (barely audible) pronounced eerie
Evidence of more to come. Roof drains rasping, moving into lower level places
Spilling the translucent moving liquid
The rivulets into roaring dirty, erratic waves
A torrent monster, unstoppable
Umbrella, roof, cover! Nature's foreboding warning, a buzzing noise
Soon ebb and flow diminish
Rain-flood, so omnipotent has its own life
Sending a message
We huddle, under cover, trying to listen to music or TV
We are aware of nature's brunt
We are dry! We are safe – for now

Than – drip – drip – ping. The gutter rattles, the window pane repels
Is it ever over?

We need you Mother Rain
In proportion, without pain
We know the sun will shine, even showers soon will end
You turn into rivers and torrential streams
This cascade from the heavens is our foe and sometimes our friend
And when men ridicule our earth
In egocentric dominating acts
Then heaven's might, a busy toll hints to neglect
A force beyond teaches us to choose and to select
And show, though belated, a new deserved respect
In humbleness and awe, some of us are wiser
Have now had that well-earned respect
Cleansed is the air
The flowers, trees are fed
It's time to say goodnight as we rest our weary heads

## *Endure-Go-Do*

A touch of hope
A pinch of smile
Eternity to cope
Life, every day a trial

Patience, forbearance, often win
Survive the ebb and flow, each wave we ride
Close with a trusted friend or kin
With love, share great support at every side

Adversity      how you perceive each changing day
Joyously partake in duty, smiling while you work
There's time to build, to laugh and cry    to pray
Rejuvenated with new rest each day,   a genuine perk

In this kaleidoscope of life
Pulled in the maelstrom, head above
All about is nature, fragrance, blessed and rife
While good luck petals rain with love

Endure the pain
The anguish, wind of destiny uncertain
You will survive, you will sustain
Another act of life    not the final curtain

Sometimes to blindly face the hour
Do what you do     cause it is just and right
Your strength, your energy still tower
You will accomplish and succeed with humble pride

Go out and do, now that you've had your rest
Participate and live
Win or lose, there is nothing but the best
You will receive, be blessed      rewarded as you give

## Dead Love

Will my dear departed love in dream intrude
As I recline to sleep
An eerie mood
Here angels dwell and reap
Desires for fulfillment mount
Fulfill me, stave off my anxiety
Strong sexual feelings do count
She was a dear, my lovely one

Why had she suffered so much
Why all the agony, pain and such
Leaving me here to mourn
I love you still on your sojourn
So please now let me sleep
Serenity I want to reap
Let me enjoy the sensual pleasures
Which do abate as time, as nature measures

Good night
Sensations never stop
Here at the zenith with you
With other      not the same    I flop

I see you still
Always will
In visions of my mind
Left me pining        far behind

## Words Kill

Some of us are too direct
Words are like bullets, kill
Instead of the slow water torture
Smooth careful
Still they kill

## The Other Side of Happiness

Everyone lusts, craves sometimes
It's the other side of happiness and joy
Our life not always poetry and rhymes
We are pitted against nature, health and ploy

Avoid the pain and smile
Search, plan the festive inner peace
Our body's up and down ebb in their style
Though we do care, there's nature
Doing not to please

Out from inner sanctum into space
Into the world of play, work, travel
Topple the mountains, world below we face
Adversity, sickness, rejection we unravel

Wounded, we soon heal
Never to return as we were
Only we know how we feel
Move on, our inner juices stir
Crave and lust
Because we must
Live
Until we die

# Simply...

this is not the final day

or...               the last day of my life
                            on earth

or...               a continuum of stratified

or...                  rarified, satisfied

        it simply is
        simply was

        it is                 regret
                          scare
                                fright

worry  (concern)

it is the party, fun free love

            for what all cavemen

                                        yearn

# Silent Prayer

When we are blessed
Faith surrounds us
Some mighty spirit envelopes
Protects us
In the form of silent prayer

When we write we reveal
When we proclaim yes or no
When we pray in awe we kneel
Our values, prejudice show

We are a reflection
Of our upbringing, of our birth
We are that human imperfection
That over/under what we value is our worth

When someday we total our deeds on earth
When love, family, work save the treasure
Underlie what we are worth
It's a big bill, too late to recoup in measure

So in a ghostly form we come and go
Some that we mined, it's better we don't know
So with energy, enthusiasm, show respect
It's time to take a breather, dwell with nature and collect

Imagine, stand so natural naked pure
Our temporary voyage here on earth to take a cure
All of us special, gifted in a thousand ways
Build on our knowledge and perception phase by phase

We are alive in many forms
We taste and test and tease life's norms
Rejoice and plan on next to come
Fatigued at end of day, so close eyes, body numb

What reason, what mission
Rejuvenation, children revision
Like ants on earth's crust
We do it 'cause we must

Yet in mind a rumbling noise
Get hold, get hold
We do have choice